THIS BOOK BELONGS TO:

....

For my beautiful children Annuska, Maikaa and Phoenix.
You are my inspiration, my life, my everything.
Thank you for the music, the magic and the mystery you bring.

Are We Really That Different? © Chandni Sethi 2022

Written by Chandni Sethi
Illustrated by Conille Felias

ISBN: 978-1-922717-09-2 (paperback)

Published by Rainbow Express Publishing and InHouse Publishing.
www.inhousepublishing.com.au

Printed in Australia by InHouse Print & Design.

A catalogue record for this book is available from the National Library of Australia

www.rainbowexpresspublishing.com
www.freestylekids.com.au
Facebook: @arewereallythatdifferent   Instagram: @are_we_really_that_different

Inspiration!

I was inspired to write this book for my kids and all the other kids in the world that may feel different or are made to feel different because of the colour of their skin. The idea sparked after an incident where my little ones, at age four, were told they weren't invited to a classmate's birthday party because of their skin colour. I was deeply saddened and shocked that something like this could happen in this day and age. It was so disheartening for me to witness the insecurities creep up in my children afterwards.

We are not born with prejudice or bias. These are, unfortunately, learned. It's about time we change these misconceptions in people young and old. It's never too late! Thus, we set forth to bring this message out into the world. In 2020, with the "Black Lives Matter" movement taking centre stage, and the first COVID lockdown, I was determined to make an impact and reach as many people as possible.

The book is titled "Are We Really That Different?" My wish is that children all around the world can see themselves as being the same as other kids despite their colour differences and celebrate their individuality in their own unique ways.

It's partly written in rhyme (with the help of my little rhymers Annuska & Maikaa) and touches on topics of kindness, love, compassion, inclusion, acceptance, fun, and laughter.

I'm a mum of three

Just happy to be me.

I live by the sea

in a house full of glee.

Our life is a song

Of love and laughter,

Craziness and chatter!

Together, we stand strong.

This is exactly

Where I belong!

Why We Love It!

"Through my many years' experience in education I understand the power of a good book. A cleverly written story will be enjoyed on many levels. Chandni's rhyming story – *Are We Really That Different?* is such a book. Children thoroughly enjoyed it as a shared story experience. This was evidenced by the smiles on their faces, the laughter in their voices and their high levels of engagement. Equally as important is this book's ability to be used as a springboard for building individual character and positive school culture, which in turn can be used to make the world a better place. I thoroughly recommend it."

– **Dr Lyn Bishop OAM**, Founder and Former Principal/CEO of Sheldon College.

"I have used Chandni's book to help children reflect on the benefits of inclusive behaviours – benefits to others and benefits to themselves. The children really connected with the message because of the light-hearted nature of the language and because they weren't being hit over the head with the message. This more subtle and nuanced approach is always way more effective and sticks with the children long term. I wouldn't be surprised if this is a text that they revisit with fondness throughout their older lives. The rhymes are delightful – and not overly predictable - eliciting all shades of emotion during the shared story telling. The beautiful illustrations capped everything off nicely. This is a book to be enjoyed on multiple levels on many different occasions."

– **Rick Samuels**, Director of Community Engagement of Sheldon College.

"This book is a must read... It's guaranteed to warm your heart and feed your soul."

– **Michelle Luhrmann**, Early childhood Teacher.

"Chandni has written this children's book with a beautiful message of love and value. The artwork shows children of all nationalities accepting each other with love and kindness. The book has a rhythm and beat all of its own telling a powerful message of friends and family and oneness within our world."

– **Bernadette Barr**, Lmus.A, Australian Kodaly Specialist.

Are We Really That DIFFERENT?

Chandni Sethi

Illustrated by Conille Felias

We may look different,
yet we are the same.

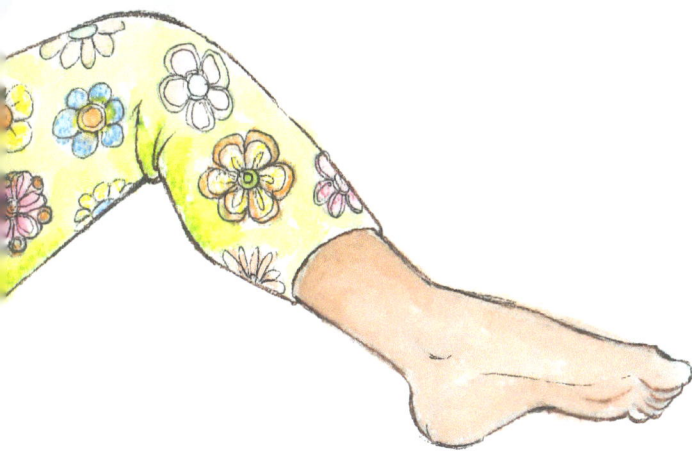

We have a body with arms and legs.
We have fingers, toes, hands and feet.
We have eyes, ears, lips, and a nose,
with skin from head to toe.

Do you have the same?
Dark or light, it doesn't matter, you know.

We have a heart that beats.
We have a brain that thinks.
We have lungs to breathe.
We have muscles and bones
and so much more.
Our bodies are amazing,
don't you know?

Doesn't matter
about our colour.

We are having fun together!

We are happy little chappies
and cheeky little monkeys.

SEE what we do ...

We sit, we stand,
we use our hands.

We walk, we talk,
we draw with chalk.

We tap, we clap,
our fingers we snap.

We flip, we flop,
we jump
to the top.

We swing, we sway,
we sing every day.

We prance, we glance,
we try a new dance.

Pirates and princesses,
    fairies and superheroes.
We just want to play
    dress-up every day!

We skip, we hop,
we don't like to stop.

We bounce, we pounce,
we learn to pronounce.

We ride, we glide,
we zoom down the slide.

We run, we swim,
we fill life to the brim.

We kick, we catch,
we play a match.

We sashay and say "yay" as we
just want to stay and PLAY!

We count, we peek,
we play hide and seek.

We wiggle, we giggle
as we get a tickle.

We scream, we shout,
we laugh out loud.

We write, we read,
we thread some beads.

We craft, we paint,
we love life so quaint.

We cook, we clean,
we eat our greens.

We say "Hip, hip, hooray!"
and celebrate
our birthday.

We hug, we kiss,
our friends we miss.

We care, we share,
we are all precious
and rare.

We are loving, we are kind,
we are sweet and
have a clever mind.

We hold hands in prayer
and thank God for his love and care.

To fall asleep,
we count sheep,
and dream dreams
ever so sweet.

Black or white, yellow or brown.
It doesn't matter, you know.
We are all special. It's more fun this way!
Did you know we are born pure and kind and true?
God made us all this way.
So I can be me and you can be you.
TOGETHER, we are the SAME.

We all have feelings,
don't you know?
I have feelings
you have feelings.

So, don't judge me. Don't call me names.
Don't pick on me. Don't hurt me.
I have feelings, just like you.
I feel pain too. I feel sad too.
I feel lonely too.

SO, let's be friends.
Here, take my hand ...

Let's climb trees
and jump in autumn leaves.
Listen to birds singing tunes
and slide down sandy dunes.

Spy a rainbow in the sky
after the rain has shimmered by.
Gaze up at the twinkling stars,
dreaming away a few hours.

Like the colours of a rainbow, together we glisten and glow. All around the world:
AUSTRALIA to SOUTH AMERICA, EUROPE to AFRICA, ASIA to NORTH AMERICA and ANTARCTICA.

All as one. One heart. One love.

We are all BEAUTIFUL.
We are all POWERFUL.
We are all JOYFUL.

Let all our colours sing together in perfect harmony as ONE VOICE.

Are We Really That Different?

We May Look Different Yet We Are The Same We have a body with arms and legs We have fingers toes hands and feet We have eyes ears lips and a nose with skin from head to toe Do you have the same? Dark or light it doesn't matter you know We have a heart that beats we have a brain that thinks we have lungs to breathe We have muscles and bones and so much more Our bodies are amazing don't you know? Doesn't matter about our colour we are having fun together

Music by Bernadette Barr

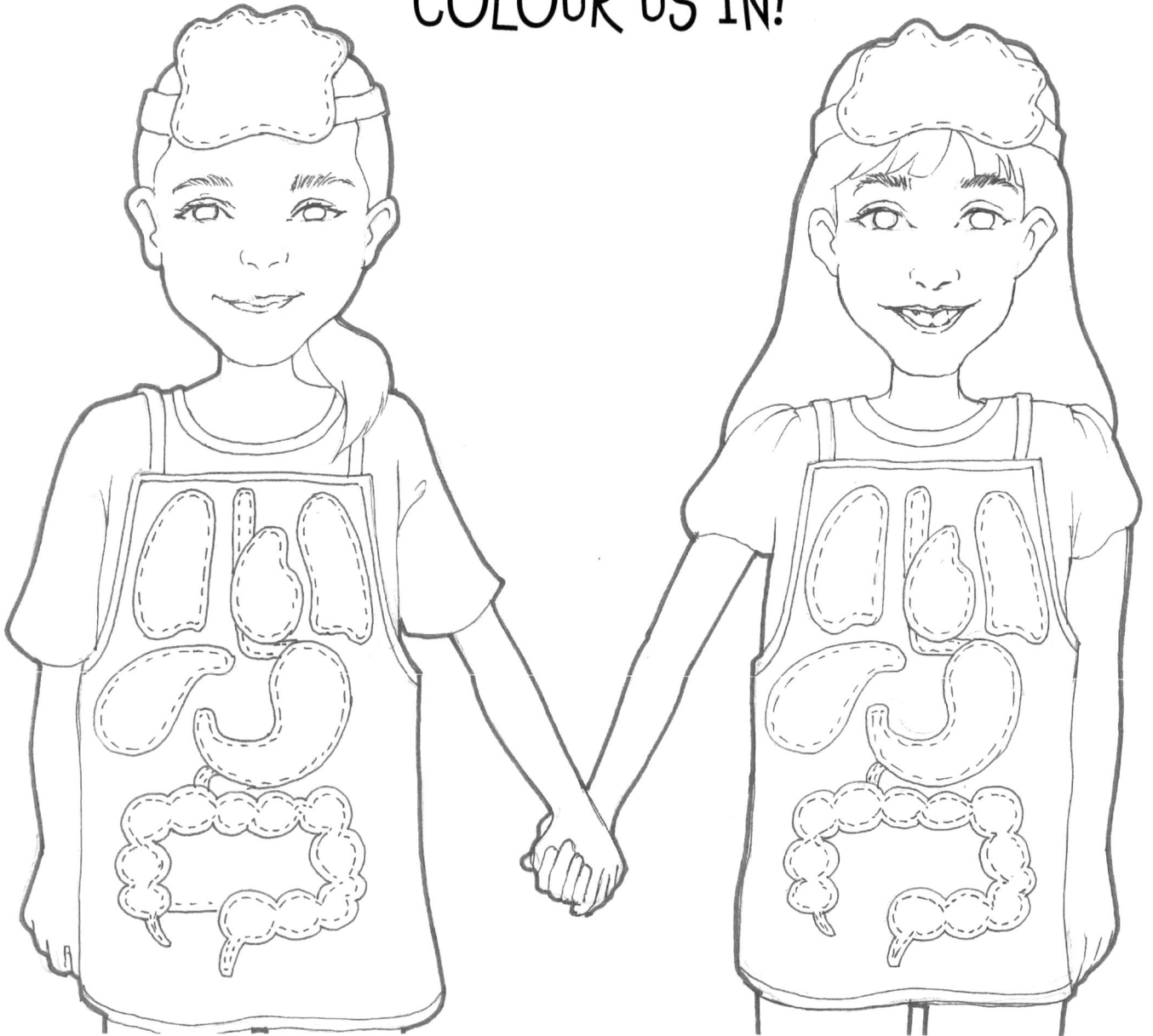

COLOUR US IN!

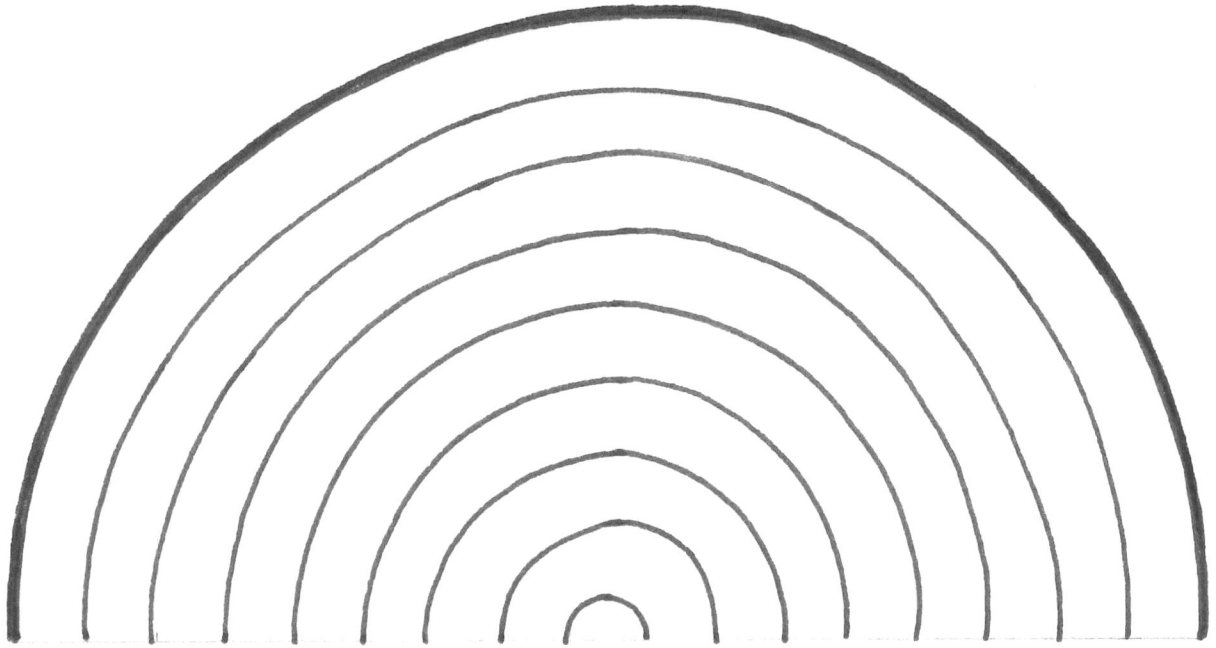

FIND THE WORDS!

S	Q	T	V	X	W	H	P
R	Z	F	U	N	C	E	E
A	L	E	N	P	J	A	A
I	O	M	I	K	I	R	C
N	V	I	L	E	D	T	E
B	E	K	I	N	D	H	J
O	I	N	D	A	F	T	O
W	H	A	R	M	O	N	Y

WORD SEARCH

RAINBOW

LOVE

HARMONY

KIND

HEART

PEACE

JOY

Art by Conille!

Conille Felias is an artist and mother who lives in the Northern Beaches of Sydney, Australia. She was born in Manila, Philippines, and graduated from the University of Santo Tomas with a Bachelor of Fine Arts. She worked at Fil-Cartoons Animation Studio and Moving Images from 1989 to 1993, prior to coming to Australia.

Conille was sponsored by Walt Disney Animation Australia and worked at the company from 1994 to 2006. Conille used her exceptional drawing skills as part of a team that created hand drawn animated movies prior to the introduction of 3D animations, which is an experience that she cherishes.

The closure of Walt Disney Animation Australia in 2006 allowed Conille to be a stay-at-home mother, able to spend time with her 3 beautiful kids. She now works as an Art Teacher at Mona Vale School of Visual Arts. She also helps out with the administration work at her husband's Accounting Practice.

No matter how busy life gets, Conille always makes sure she has time to create her own artworks. She believes art nurtures the soul.

www.ingramcontent.com/pod-product-compliance
Lightning Source LLC
LaVergne TN
LVHW072054070426
835508LV00002B/97